INVASION OF THE CLUB

By
D.A. McCall
Heidie McCall

Have you had your shots?

FUN ART

Factory West Studio
is a multi-media production company
a place where "Art Is Fun."

www.factoryweststudio.com
Email: hm@factoryweststudio.com
Factory West Studio Est. 1985

DEDICATION

The book is dedicated to Pogo,
a sagacious dog who would have,
with perplexed bewilderment,
posed the question, "Why am I here?"
The occasion's magic
would have completely eluded her.

Top Dogs

DOUG: Doug writes under the pen name of D.A. McCall. D.A.'s last book is "The Family Album."

Doug says, "The great Bob Costas was tracked down and sent a copy of the tome. In an unexpected phone call Bob was very gracious in his comments and expressed sincere gratitude that he'd been thought of. In contacting Bob I'm unsure what my expectations had been. Perhaps a quote I could use on the jacket to boost sales. Now that this seemed a possibility I put myself in the shoes of a would be buyer.

"I don't know. I think the book's about baseball." Hmmmm, I guess I'll just go with name dropping."

HEIDIE: A visionary artist (with a nod toward Nostradamus) Heidie foresaw many of today's standards. An almost insulting partial list includes flavored coffee creamers, shampoo with built-in conditioner, she even predated YouTube with Surf TV™.

These days Heidie is most passionate about Human Energy. "Human Energy is the solution to the world's most vexing ills."

Heidie's most recent prediction is, "The day will come when funerals are broadcast twenty-four hours a day. (Farewell TV). Everybody loves a funeral."

If this contention is true, my guess is that it reminds them that they are still alive.

Introduction

The Southwest Washington Humane Society held its third annual "Doggie Dive" at the Lake Shore Athletic Club (Vancouver, Washington).

On the final day of the outdoor swim season, the two pools are reserved for the dogs. All dogs are welcome for a ten-dollar donation. The 2009 edition of the "Doggie Dive" attracted one hundred and seventy (mostly) enthusiastic participants. The event raised over $2500.00 for the Humane Society.

If the occasion's previous attendees could talk, all summer they'd chorus a relentless refrain of "Can we go to the pool now? Can we go to the pool now?"

For one of the few days in the life of a dog, the canines romp and play unrestrained by the vice grips of obedience training. The pooches' unbridled joy is palpable.

Heidie McCall's photographs sublimely captured the day.

With no small regret, I didn't use the images of all the dogs that participated.

Politics played no role in this slight. It's just that there are only so many poses (even the most photogenic) that a dog in a pool of water can achieve.

I must confess that even the photos I did choose for this project often had elusive narratives. If you'd read one of my early interpretations you might have said, "I think he captured the picture better with that caption." The thing is, you weren't here, and I didn't.

Acknowledgment

With Bobbie Nelson there was no
conflicted muse. Bobbie's genius
is prominently displayed on every page.
Thank you seems inadequate.
I'll say it anyway, thank you.

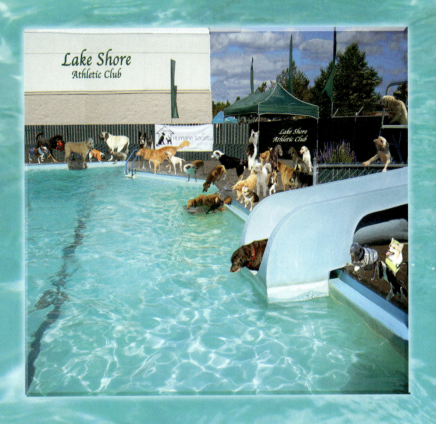

"Let's make the water turn black."

– Frank Zappa

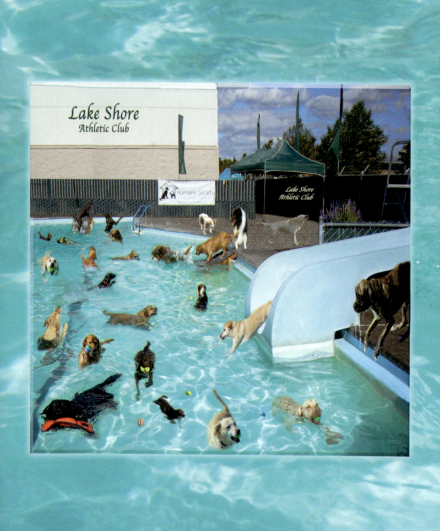

"You call this a lake?"

With Lassie there are three stipulations:
All photographs must be of her good side,
soft focus, Lassie doesn't do water.

"Did you ever see Michael Phelps
dog paddle with a ball in his mouth?
I didn't think so."

"I'm biting the next chump who says, this place has really gone to the dogs."

"I can't believe I forgot my goggles."

"If I'm color blind, how do you suppose I found the purple ball?"

" I learned how to swim watching Saturday morning cartoons."

Color coordinated perfect form.

"Don't pay any attention
to him, that's what he wants."

"I can't believe I forgot my snorkel."

Synchronized swimming

"I knew there was a ball in my ear."

"I was misinformed. I fail to see any ducks."

"This ain't easy without my glasses."

"A reliable source
informed me that
the pool has been
stocked with piranha."

The intoxicating aroma of a wet dog.

"I can't believe I forgot
my swim cap."

"Huh-uh there's nothing in my mouth."

"To think I once lived for this."

"Salt & pepper shakers, I don't get it?"

"I can do this with my eyes closed."

"I've got my eye on you."

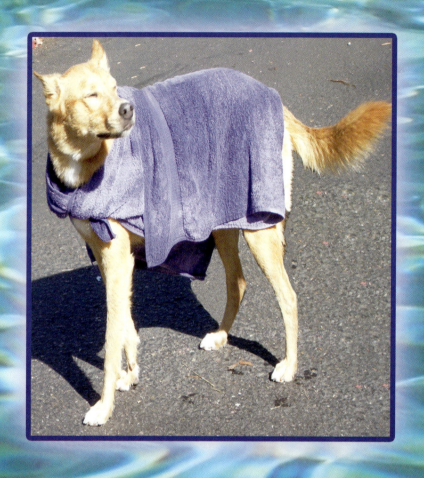

"I knew I should have worn my shades."

"It's impolite to say,
'Look at those eyes,'
about someone with goiter."

"I'm fine, why do you ask?"

The argument for cloning.

"Just follow me you said,
so where are the steps?"

"I just saw my reflection.
Damn I'm gorgeous."

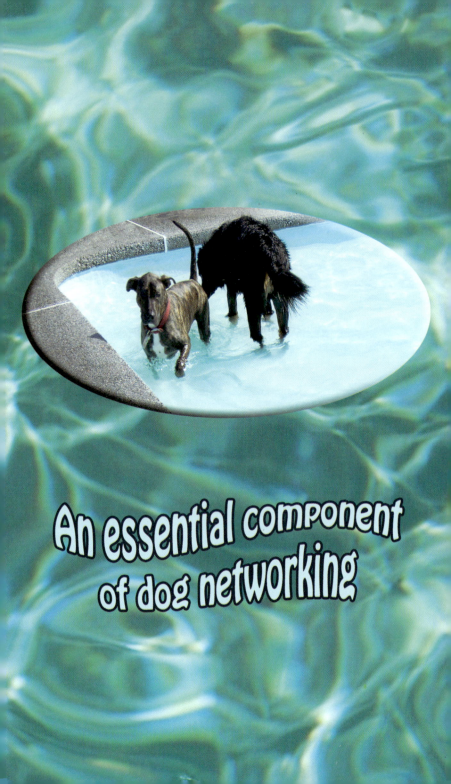

An essential component
of dog networking

"You lied,
you said there wouldn't be any water this year."

"Who had the bright idea to put the tennis court next to the swimming pool anyway?"

"I know it can't be but,
this sure seems like the same ball."

A rare moment when every dog
had at least one tennis ball.

"There just aren't many motors like mine."

"I knew I'd be glad I brought my fins."

"Spit your little brother out, right now!"

"That's easy for you to say,
you're wearing a life jacket."

"The water just can't be good for my fats."

"Back off."

"This ain't no water moccasin.
You just want me to let go."

"Are these things breeding?"

"Rookies just don't stay in their lanes."

"Throw the ball again and I'll kill you."

The participants in mixed doubles tennis.

"I'm getting waterlogged."

"It's a good thing I read the sign before I got water in my eyes."

"Don't even think about it."

"What do you suppose is floating out there?"

"I'm not putting that ball in my mouth, it's completely wrapped up with dog slobber."

"I'm getting too old for this."

"Just as many had feared,
these things had become air-borne."

"Is this a case of bad breeding,
or are you always this pushy?"

"You don't want to know."

"Don't ever slip up behind me."

"Alright, there really are two balls.
I thought it was just my double vision flaring up."

"I fail to see the logic of no hands,
no hand rail?"

Gigi was drawn to a camera
like a bee to honey.

"You want the ball? You get it."

Old dogs, new tricks, what a combination.

"I'd like to go for a swim but,
I've just come from the hairdressers."

"I don't think so."

"You can run but you can't hide."

"What's water?"

"I may have hair in my eyes but, I know what I see."

"Did you see that?"

A spirited game of tennis ball tag.

"That's disgusting, besides we just met."

"Isn't it time to go yet?"

"Enough already."

"That's it. I'm leaving."

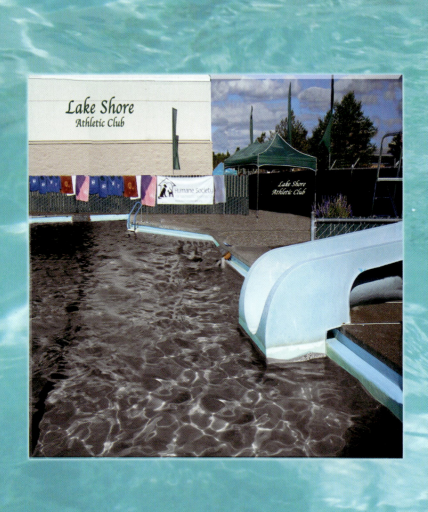